Researching Events

Maity Schrecengost

Alleyside Press®

Fort Atkinson, Wisconsin

Contents

Published by Alleyside Press, an imprint of Highsmith Press
W5527 Highway 106
P.O. Box 800
Fort Atkinson, Wisconsin 53538-0800   **1-800-558-2110**

© S. Maitland Schrecengost, 1998
Cover design: Frank Neu

The paper used in this publication meets the minimum requirements of American National Standard for Information Science — Permanence of Paper for Printed Library Material. ANSI/NISO Z39.48-1992.

Library of Congress Cataloging-in-Publication Data

Schrecengost, Maity, 1938–
     Researching events / Maity Schrecengost.
       p. cm.
     Includes bibliographical references.
     Summary: An introductory guide to using library resources for a
research paper on historical or contemporary events.
     ISBN: 1-57950-018-8 (pbk.)
     1. History–Research–Juvenile literature. 2. History–
Methodology–Juvenile literature. 3. Report writing–Juvenile
literature. [1. History–Research. 2. History–Methodology.
3. Report writing. 4. Research.] I. Title.
D13.S397 1998
907'.2–dc21   98-15431
           CIP

Materials in **Researching Events** were used with permission from:

Chapter 6. Sample index entry from *Magazine Index Plus.* ©1997, Information Access Company.

Chapter 7. *Fact-Index*, example index page (p. 112), and *Challenger* Space Shuttle article (S-478) from *Compton's Encyclopedia.* (© 1997 Encyclopedia Britannica Corp.)

Chapter 10. Article by Eydie Cubarrubia, "Are We Spaced Out?" *Bradenton Herald* (August 31, 1997) People Section, p. 3; and Letter to the Editor by June Clark; *Bradenton Herald* (August 17, 1997) Editorial Section, p. 4. *Bradenton Herald.*

Chapter 11. Article by Jay Hamburg from the *Orlando Sentinel* (February 9, 1986) p. A-16. (©1986, *Orlando Sentinel.* Text by Richard S. Lewis from *Challenger: The Final Voyage.* p. 3. (©1988 Columbia University Press).

Getting Started

Hitler Invades Poland! President Kennedy Fatally Wounded! Mount St. Helen Erupts! Berlin Wall Crumbles! *Challenger* Explodes! Bombing Terrorizes Oklahoma City! Hurricane Andrew Devastates Homestead! Princess Diana Dies in Fiery Crash!

Years ago, newsboys stood on busy street corners calling, "Extra! Extra! Read all about it! Get your newspaper here," while waving papers whose headlines blared the news-making events of the day.

Today, in addition to newspapers, headline news events are carried on radio, on television via satellite, and on our personal computers by way of the Internet. Yet despite the greater range in media used to deliver these stories, the same kinds of events still make headline news.

Events are happenings. But not all happenings are newsworthy. For example, the day of your birth was an important happening in the life of your family. But, unless you are one of a set of quadruplets, the son or daughter of a celebrity, or unusual circumstances surrounded your birth, it is unlikely that your birth made front-page news.

Headline events may be defined as:

Newsworthy happenings of widespread interest that affect the lives and/or feelings of a large number of people.

What kinds of events make headline news?

Some major headline news events are those that ...

Changed the course of history.

World Wars I and II, the end of communism in the Soviet Union, the bombing of Pearl Harbor, and the bringing down of the Berlin Wall are examples of such world-changing events.

Became historic moments.

Other events, such as the signing of the Declaration of Independence, the Confederate Army's firing on Fort Sumter initiating the Civil War, the battle of the Alamo, or Neil Armstong's first step upon the moon, were destined to become **Historic Moments**.

Hurricane Andrew, the eruption of Mount St. Helen, the Johnstown Flood, earthquakes, and other **Natural Disasters** are all too often headline news-events.

And so are **Man-made Calamities** like kidnappings, mass murders, assassinations of national or world leaders, or terrorist bombings.

Involved famous people or

Some events are newsworthy because they involve **Well-known Personalities.** The disappearance of Amelia Earhart, the kidnapping of the Lindbergh baby, the assassinations of Martin Luther King and John F. Kennedy, the drowning at Chappaquidick, and the tragic death of Princess Diana are several that come to mind.

An unsolved mystery.

Events may make headlines because they are **Mysterious** — for example, alleged UFO sightings or reports of the appearance of Bigfoot.

Recorded the actions of courts of law, or

Famous Court Trials and Decisions are rich fodder for newspaper reporters. The Scopes Trial, the Dred Scott Decision, and more recently, the O. J. Simpson murder trial were headline news events of the day.

Followed the highs and lows of sports teams or personalities.

Events in the **World of Sports** may not make front page news, but will surely be headlines in the sports section. The disqualification of Pete Rose from professional sports for a gambling violation, and Jackie Robinson's entrance into major league baseball were both news-makers.

Finally, there are events that are regional...

That is, they are mainly of interest to people who live in a certain region of the country. But they are still newsworthy events. For example, the Little League Team in the city I call home won the Eastern Division and went on to play in the Little League World Series in Williamsport, Pennsylvania. You better believe this event made daily headline news in our local papers right up to the day the boys came home after capturing second place!

This is certainly not a complete list of all possible types of news-making events, but these examples should stimulate your thinking as you begin to consider events for the topic of your research project.

As you think about topics, keep in mind the definition of a headline event:

A newsworthy happening of widespread interest that affects the lives and/or feelings of a large number of people.

Choosing Your Topic

Research is more than gathering information. It also involves making choices and decisions about that information: what information will be selected and how the information will be used. The first and most important decision you will make is the choice of an appropriate topic. You will, of course, choose a topic that is within the assignment guidelines set by your teacher.

Consider these as you work through the process of choosing your topic.

1. Does the topic meet the definition of a newsworthy event?

2. Is the topic interesting to you personally?

3. Will you have adequate sources of information?

4. Does the topic fall within the requirements of the assignment?

Your teacher may assign an event from this decade. Or the assignment may be limited to a specific area, such as natural disasters.

Focus on a topic

Focus on Challenger Disaster As I thought about topics I might use for demonstrating research skills, I thought of many possibilities. I chose the Challenger disaster over the others for several reasons.

1. First, it fits the definition of a newsworthy event that I used in chapter 1: "a newsworthy happening ... of widespread interest ... that effected change in the lives and/or feelings of people." Certainly everyone in the U.S., if not the whole world, was aware of the tragedy and attitudes toward space flight were strongly effected.

2. Second, the topic interests me because a teacher was on board the Challenger. Because I, too, am a teacher, I have a personal interest in the topic.

3. Finally, since the event took place here in Florida where I live, I can find a variety of sources from newspapers to eyewitness interviews.

Once you have made your choice, what's next?

Having chosen a topic, you must now narrow it to fit within the length of a research paper. If you have chosen well, there will be newspaper and magazine articles, news reports and even books about your topic. It will be impossible to cover everything, so now, at the beginning, it is important to focus on just one or two aspects of the event.

Narrow your focus

Focus on *Challenger* Disaster As I consider the topic, several approaches come to mind. I could research the cause or causes of the explosion. I could focus on Christa McAuliffe's involvement in the disaster. Or I could investigate the events that took place just prior to the explosion. What was happening inside the space craft? Another idea might be to examine the effect the *Challenger's* explosion had on the space program.

▶ You need to focus on your selected topic in the same way. It's far better to have a narrower scope and do a thorough investigation, than to have a broad topic and treat it superficially. Look at your chosen subject carefully, keeping in mind the scope and length of the assigned project and narrow it to a workable topic.

Creating a **mind map or web** can help you see the Big Picture. Brainstorming like this is a good way to get down all the things you already know—or want to know—about your event.

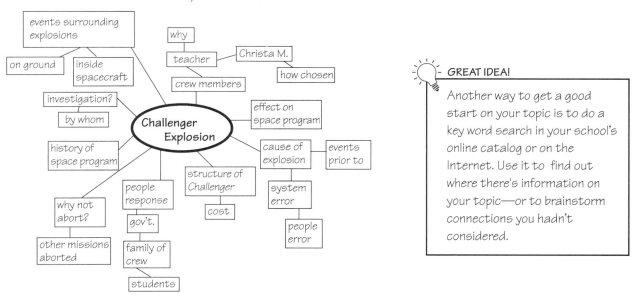

GREAT IDEA!

Another way to get a good start on your topic is to do a key word search in your school's online catalog or on the Internet. Use it to find out where there's information on your topic—or to brainstorm connections you hadn't considered.

When you have chosen and focused on your topic, you are ready to prepare to begin your research.

Planning for the Research

Seasoned travelers know that setting out on a long trip without a road map can have disastrous results: ***wrong turns, detours, and lots of frustration.*** The same is true for a big project like a research paper. In order to avoid confusion, you will want to take some time to map out your research plans—in this case **a calendar is going to be your guide**.

You need to include your starting date and more importantly, the due date. Schedule the approximate time(s) for starting and completing each step in the research process. Creating a calendar like the one below will give direction to your work and keep you on schedule so that you will arrive at the Due Date on time with a finished project in hand.

Calendar

April

Sun.	Mon.	Tues.	Wed.	Thur.	Fri.	Sat.
28	29 Choose topic!	30 Make Schedule	31 Prepare Questions	1 Tour media ctr.	2 ✱ Scout Banquet!	3 Softball practice
4	5 Begin research	6 Softball	7 Research Math Test	8 Finish lib. research	9 School Dance	10 Public Lib. research
11 Mom's B-day!	12 Other Sources	13 Other Sources	14 Scouts study for history test	15 Softball	16 Organize notes	17 Begin rough draft
18 Church picnic	19 Finish 1st draft	20 Softball	21 Ask Jack to read paper	22 Revise 1st draft	23 Make bibliography	24 Begin last draft
25	26 Finish paper	27 Research Paper due!	28 scouts	29 Book report due!	30	1

▼

Middle school students are busy people. Your days are filled with many different kinds of activities. As you plan your schedule, write in those activities. Remember to put in family and social events as well as your responsibilities for other school subjects.

A well-planned trip allows time to explore unexpected points of interest along the way. Be sure to include time for "detours" in your schedule. As you do your research, you will surely come across articles, books, or Web sites that capture your interest. You'll want to look them over for background information. If you're pressed for time, you won't be able to do this, and may miss out on some valuable information. Even though you may not directly use all the information you find, the background knowledge you have will add richness and depth to your report.

Know where you want to go!

In the same way a calendar keeps you on schedule, you need other helps to keep you going in the right direction as you do your research.

Preparing a list of questions before you go to the media center or library will give direction to your investigation. It will serve as another guide to help keep you from making wrong turns, chasing useless information up blind alleys.

If I focus on Christa McAuliffe's role in the space mission, the cause of the explosion, and the effect her death as a civilian had on the space program, I won't be investigating the costs of the mission, the structure of the *Challenger*, the history of the space program, previous shuttle missions, or personal details about the other astronauts — although I will come across that information in my background reading.

Questions

My list of questions might look something like this:

Why were civilians included in this space mission?

Why was Christa McAuliffe chosen?

What were her qualifications?

What was McAuliffe's role on the mission?

Who were the other astronauts?

Which of the astronauts were civilians?

How did McAuliffe's family feel about her space flight?

How were McAuliffe's students involved in her participation?

Why wasn't the flight aborted?

What impact did the disaster have on McAuliffe's students?

Could the disaster have been prevented?

What impact did the disaster have on the space program?

This is not a final list of questions. During the research, other questions will come to mind and they will be added to the list. But having an initial list will be helpful as you begin wading through the wealth of information written about your topic. Since you have a focus for the report, you'll be less tempted to wander aimlessly through the reams of material you'll find—and more able to get back on topic if a hypertext link leads you far astray.

After your list is completed, write each question at the top of a 3"x5" or 4"x6" note card. Or you may write each question at the top of a notebook page; one question to a page. (I prefer to use note cards because they make organizing the information easier when I am ready to write the first draft). When you take your notes, you will write the answer(s) to the question on your note card or notebook page, remembering to write down the source of the information and the page on which you found it.

Answers

Who were the *Challenger* crew members?

Francis R. (Dick) Scobee

Michael John Smith, pilot

Ellison S. Onizuka, mission specialist one

Judith Arlene Resnik, mission specialist two

Ronald Erwin McNair, mission specialist three

S. Christa McAuliffe, payload specialist one

Gregory Bruce Jarvis, payload specialist two

Lewis, Dedication page

Outline

Now you need an OUTLINE

To further organize your ideas, you may use the list of questions to write an early outline for your report. The outline may remind you of additional questions. At this point, the outline will be very general. It can't be specific because you don't know yet what information you will find.

Outline

An early outline for a report on the *Challenger* Disaster: Christa McAuliffe might look like this:

I. Background Information

    A. What was the Challenger's mission?

    B. When and where did it occur?

II. Civilian Involvement

    A. Why were civilians involved?

    B. Who were the civilians involved?

III. Christa McAuliffe--Astronaut

    A. What were her qualifications?

    B. What was her role in the mission?

IV. McAuliffe--Personal Background

    A. What led to her decision to take part in the mission?

    B. Did her family support her decision?

    C. What role did her school and students play?

V. The Disaster

    A. Cause/causes of the disaster

    B. Could the disaster have been avoided?

    C. What was the effect on McAuliffe's family and students?

VI. Effect on Space Program

    A. Were new safe-guards put in place?

    B. Were there fewer missions?

▶ This is not a finished outline, of course. A general outline like this can help direct your search. As you do the research, you may find additional information that you want to include. A look at your outline will let you know if and where the information will fit. Perhaps you will modify your outline to include the new information and that's fine, too.

Now that you have a well-planned schedule for starting, conducting, and completing your research journey, you are ready to pack your research bag. What will you need? Pencils and note cards, for sure. A notebook or maybe a laptop computer. The calendar, questions, and outline you have prepared will guide you through the rest of your research journey.

Touring the Media Center

A review of how libraries are organized will make your visits there more efficient and profitable. The library resources you will read about in the next several chapters all fit into three broad groupings based on their format—or the way in which the information is delivered to us. These three are: Print Resources, Non-Print Resources, and Electronic Resources. We'll begin our library tour with the books and other print sources that you see every time you enter the library.

▶ **Print Resources** are the most visible resources in the library.

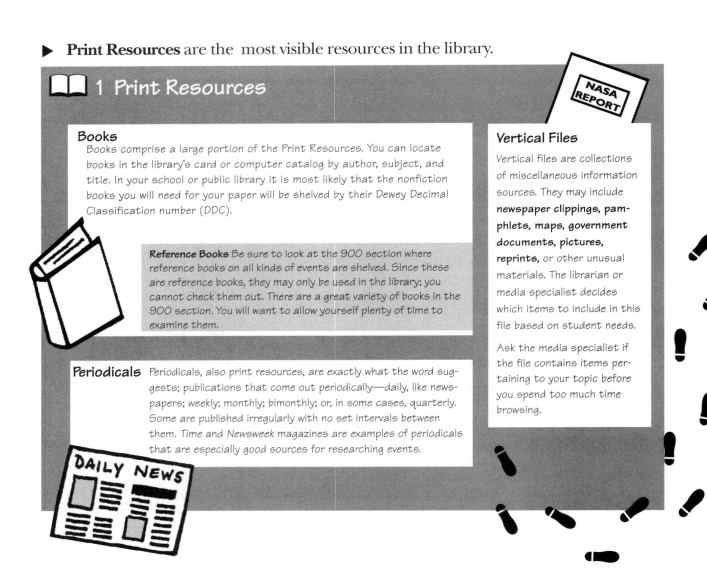

📖 1 Print Resources

Books
Books comprise a large portion of the Print Resources. You can locate books in the library's card or computer catalog by author, subject, and title. In your school or public library it is most likely that the nonfiction books you will need for your paper will be shelved by their Dewey Decimal Classification number (DDC).

Reference Books Be sure to look at the 900 section where reference books on all kinds of events are shelved. Since these are reference books, they may only be used in the library; you cannot check them out. There are a great variety of books in the 900 section. You will want to allow yourself plenty of time to examine them.

Periodicals
Periodicals, also print resources, are exactly what the word suggests; publications that come out periodically—daily, like newspapers; weekly; monthly; bimonthly; or, in some cases, quarterly. Some are published irregularly with no set intervals between them. *Time* and *Newsweek* magazines are examples of periodicals that are especially good sources for researching events.

Vertical Files

Vertical files are collections of miscellaneous information sources. They may include **newspaper clippings, pamphlets, maps, government documents, pictures, reprints,** or other unusual materials. The librarian or media specialist decides which items to include in this file based on student needs.

Ask the media specialist if the file contains items pertaining to your topic before you spend too much time browsing.

Next, you will visit the area of the library set aside for **Non-Print Resources**.

2 Non-Print Resources

Audiotapes	Laser Discs	Film Strips	Transparencies

Microforms
Because newspapers and magazines are too bulky to store and newsprint yellows and breaks down quickly, libraries keep current issues on file and store selected items from past issues on microfilm or microfiche. Usually the viewers are connected to a printer so that you may print out selected articles. Microforms are generally found only in public or university libraries.

Videotapes

The final stop on your tour is the area devoted to **Electronic Resources**.

3 Electronic Resources

OPAC

CD-ROM (Compact Disc, Read-Only Memory)
A CD-ROM stores an incredible amount of information in a small space. Whole sets of encyclopedias and entire dictionaries can be stored on one CD-ROM, saving vast amounts of shelf space. For that reason, more and more CD-ROMs are appearing in libraries or media centers. Guides are available in most libraries that describe the contents and search techniques for CD-ROMs.

Computers & Internet Access
Many computers are purchased with electronic resources installed on the hard drive or main memory. Some of these are multimedia; they have sound, video, and graphics, as well as text. This makes it possible to link easily to the Internet and access the sound and action sites for your research.

Electronic Indexes & Databases
Of great importance to the researcher are electronic indexes and databases. Databases are collections or banks of information stored in the computer or accessible online through the Internet. They are available on many different subjects.

Web sites, search engines, portals, listservs and email
Using the Internet, a computer can give you access to several different kinds of information resources. You may locate these on your school's OPAC or on separate terminals. Of course, the quality of these resources and how they are organized will be different from one to another.

Now that you have completed your tour of the media center, you have a clear picture of the many available sources of information. You want to make good use of all of them. Your careful planning will allow you time to investigate all these sources on your research journey.

In the next chapters, you will learn more about more specialized resources for researching events; where to find them; what they contain; and how to use them.

5 Using the Materials Catalog

The catalog is usually your **first stop** in the library when researching any topic. The one in your school may be a traditional catalog listing books and media located just in your library—or it may be an electronic super highway to all the resources in your library and beyond through indexes, full-text resources, and Internet access. In this chapter, we'll talk about using the catalog to find materials in the library.

Catalogs are an organized listing of the library's resources

Library catalogs may be paper, with cards stored alphabetically in drawers, or they may be computerized and the contents displayed on computer screens. Nearly all libraries are moving toward computerization and we will sometimes refer to these electronic catalogs as **OPACS (Online Public Access Catalogs)**. In either case, this is where you will find "address" information for many of the materials in the library.

Systems for organizing materials may differ, but...

Most school libraries use the **Dewey Decimal Classification System** to organize the books they have. This is the system you are most likely to be familiar with already. The **Library of Congress (LC) System** is used by many large public and university libraries. Libraries may also use a variety of special systems for all or some of the books they have. Whatever system is used, the purpose is to help you locate the books you need.

Since everything in the library is organized by subject, you will start your search by looking up subjects or subject headings in the catalog. Libraries try to be consistent in using the same set of subject headings in their catalogs, but because some terms change, you will find cross references or "see also" references to guide you to new or related subject headings. Once you find a heading that works in one library, you should be able to use it in other libraries as well.

Subject headings

In researching the *Challenger* disaster, I might try the subjects "*Challenger*" or "*Space Missions.*" Near the end of the chosen subject description, I would see a list of other subject headings. These provide ideas for more subject headings to check for additional information.

When you locate a book or video or CD in the catalog, it will have a call number directing you to its location.

> 921
> C24

◄ The **Call Number** is this book's library address. The top number tells the classification of the book; it groups materials on the same subject together in one place. The bottom letter and numbers (called the "Cutter" number) tells where on the shelf to find the book.

Use what you know about the topic...

In a card catalog, there will be **title, author and subject** cards. If you are using an electronic catalog, your search options will be greater. You may search for the listing in a variety of ways including by **title, author, subject, extended subject, key words in the subject or title, or combining several ways.**

For example, I found this listing by typing "Lewis, Richard S." A second time I entered the title: "Challenger, the final voyage." Finally I did an extended search by typing the words "Challenger, Spacecraft, Explosion." ▶

Call Number	Nonfiction	Status: Available
DYNIX#	61079	
AUTHOR	Lewis, Richard S., 1916–	
PUBLISHER	New York: Columbia Univ. Press, 1988	
DESCRIPT	249 p., [1] leaf of plates: ill.; 28 cm.	
NOTES	1) Includes bibliographical references.	
SUBJECTS	1) Challenger (Spacecraft)–Accidents	

Things to REMEMBER when using an OPAC

1. The catalog probably lists things other than books, including periodicals, recordings, films, videos, and maps. It may also list materials that are not in your school library, but are owned by other libraries in your area.

2. Computers allow you to do **keyword searches.** The computer searches the entire catalog for every occurrence of the word or words you enter. Or you may be able to combine author and title information in one search, or you may be able to enter two related words, like "Challenger" - "McAuliffe." Many offer Boolean search capability, allowing you to further refine your search by linking keywords with "or," "and," or "not." Since systems vary, and small differences can make or break your search, always read the system directions.

3. Systems differ in their capacity to print out or download information to a disk or hard copy. Again, read the directions.

 GREAT IDEA!

A researching tip. If the event you are researching happened within the past year, you are unlikely to find many books on the subject. In that case, go straight to the periodical and newspaper indexes.

Need help? Don't hesitate to ask your media specialist for assistance in locating materials and using the electronic resources. Each system is different and the best way to understand how to use new resources is to check with a librarian in that library.

Using Indexes

When you are researching events—*especially recent ones*—**your best resources** are primary sources such as newspapers and first person accounts in magazine articles. For that reason, it is important you know how to use subject guides to periodicals or indexes.

GREAT IDEA!

> Other primary sources are firsthand accounts found in diaries, speeches, and interviews.

MAGAZINES

The most well-known index is ***The Reader's Guide to Periodical Literature***. Published monthly, with an annual yearbook, the *Guide* includes listings for 238 periodicals. It is also available in a CD-ROM version, as well as versions containing summaries and the full text of the indexed articles. While smaller libraries may not have the *Reader's Guide* on their shelves, it will be available at most public and university libraries.

✔ *Check the front page of each volume for directions.*

✔ *Check the annual index for the year of the event and two to three years after the event.*

Example

A listing in the 1987 Reader's Guide shows 20 different articles devoted to the *Challenger* disaster. Because the list is broken into sub-topics— Challenger Explosion, Economic aspect, Photographs and photography, Reporters and reporting, and Suits and claims—the researcher is aided in making selections relevant to the focus chosen for the paper.

NEWSPAPERS

Newsbank. This index accesses *newspaper articles* from over 450 U.S. cities. Selected newspaper articles are reproduced in their full text on microfiche each month. Newsbank has added InfoWeb (http://www.newsbank.com) on the World Wide Web, which offers the full text of articles from over 2,000 sources. Articles contain all original charts, maps, photos and illustrations.

Another online index to over 130 daily newspapers is the **New Century Network** (http://www.newsworks.com). This index contains the full text of current newspaper articles on general news, business, lifestyles, science, technology and the arts.

MAGAZINES

There are two other indexes that may be useful for researching events. ***American Heritage 35 Year Cumulative Index*** is an index to *American Heritage*, a bimonthly magazine of history. It indexes issues from December 1954 to December 1989. Many school libraries also offer the ***National Geographic Index*** which catalogs 7,000 magazine articles.

Magazine Index Plus This is a very quick and easy-to-use CD-ROM index to periodicals which covers 400 magazines. It is part of a family of databases known as InfoTrac. These databases let you search by browsing subjects or you can combine two or more words or concepts and do an expanded search.

```
┌──────────────────────────────────────────────────────────┐
│ Database * Magazine Index Plus                             │
│ Key Words: challenger explosion                            │
│ Library: Manatee County Central Library                    │
│ Holdings: *Indicates that Library subscribes to this journal│
│ ---------------------------------------------------------- │
│    *   Remembering the Challenger. (space shuttle Challenger explosion; │
│        includes article on the two women astronauts Judith Resnick and │
│        Christa McAuliffe)                                   │
│        Ladies Home Journal, Jan 1996 v113 nl p98 (6).      │
│        Author: Kathryn Casey                               │
│        Abstract: The wife of one of the crew members aboard the ill-fated │
│        space shuttle Challenger, Cheryl McNair, relates her story of the │
│        accident.                                           │
│        Subjects: Challenger Space Shuttle Accident, 1986 – Accidents │
│        Women astronauts – Appreciation                     │
│        Space shuttles – Accidents                          │
│        Features: illustration; photograph                  │
└──────────────────────────────────────────────────────────┘
```

◀ Using Magazine Index Plus and entering the key words "challenger explosion" to do an expanded search reveals an article "Remembering the Challenger" printed in *Ladies Home Journal* in the January 1996 edition on page 98. The citation tells me the content, author and length of the article, and shows that it contains illustrations and photographs. It also gives me a list of additional subjects to browse.

 GREAT IDEA!

Always check the period of coverage listed for CD-ROM indexes to determine if the event you are researching falls between the dates indexed.

MAGAZINES & NEWSPAPERS

Notice, too, that doing the subject search on InfoTrac let me find an article that was published ten years after the event. Had I been content to use a paper index and searched only the yearbooks for the year of the event and a year or two later, I would have missed this potentially important source.

TOM is another CD-ROM InfoTrac index. It indexes 140 periodicals from 1985 to date. Of those, 30 are available in full text on CD-ROM. Two new versions are now available—**SuperTOM**, which is a large collection of magazine and newspaper articles in full text for high school students, and **SuperTOM, Jr.**, a version for middle school students.

Getting the article in your hands

When your index search uncovers articles that interests you, you need to find out whether the library owns the magazines or newspapers they're in, and if the articles are available in print or are stored on microfilm or microfiche. After you've checked the periodical shelves, you may need to fill out a periodical request form listing the name of the magazine, the date the article was published, and the page number where the article appears. When you take these request forms to the library staff member at the service desk, you will learn whether the articles are available and in what form.

 A good portion of your time in the library will be spent examining indexes, locating and reviewing articles, and taking useful notes. It takes lots of practice to learn to use the indexes and a long time to do a thorough search. But using the indexes will result in finding information you wouldn't find anywhere else.

Using Encyclopedias

Encyclopedias are good sources for **general information and facts**.

Not all encyclopedias are the same. Watch for date and difficulty. Your library media center probably has several sets of encyclopedias ranging from fairly easy-to-read ones that contain basic information to more complex specialized encyclopedias. Your first job is to identify the set or sets that will be most useful to you. You'll want to check the copyright dates on the back of the title pages to find out when the book was published. If you're researching a fairly recent event, it's especially important to find the most up-to-date information. Some encyclopedias indicate the date each article was written or revised, and you should look for this in the encyclopedia you select.

Two ways to find information in encyclopedias:

1. **The Easy Way**: Since encyclopedia articles are arranged alphabetically, you can locate information in the set you have chosen by selecting the volume from the set according to your subject heading. For example, I could look in the C volume for the subject heading *Challenger*.

2. **The Better Way:** The only way to locate all the information on your topic in that set of encyclopedias is by using the **index.** To do this, you need to:

Check the separate index volume...

Almost all encyclopedias will have a separate index volume which usually is the last volume in the set.

And check the front page of each volume for directions.

Each index will be slightly different so always check the directions. This sample shows part of the directions for the Fact-Index from *Compton's Encyclopedia*. The directions give you the special features of the index as well as the basic directions for understanding the entry information.

HOW TO USE THE FACT-INDEX

Always start your search for information in the Fact-Index. It is a companion to the first 25 volumes of Compton's Encyclopedia. The Fact-Index locates specific facts, illustrations, maps, and study aids by the exact volume and page. In addition, the Fact-Index contains more than 30,000 articles that are quickly found sources of facts. The many features of the Fact-Index are explained in this two-page section.

At the head of each page of the Fact-Index are the guide words. The one on the left refers to the title of the first entry to start on that page, and the one on the right refers to the title of the last entry to start on that page. The guide words and the alphabetical arrangement of all entries in the Fact-Index make it easy to find the entry for which you are looking.	The entries in the Fact-Index all start with a **boldface entry term**. These entry terms form an alphabetical list of all the people, places, and things for which you may be looking. There are three types of entries in the Fact-Index: articles, simple entries, and cross-references. **Nizhni Novgorod** is an *article* that is written in a fact-filled style. Many articles include	**Nitrogen** is a Fact-Index *article* that combines the characteristics of various types of entries. It is an article with a primary citation (16:318) and many secondary citations. There are ten alphabetically arranged secondary citations, each of which is indented one space. In some entries these citations are important enough to be broken down into alphabetically arranged tertiary citations, each of	Some of the entries are accompanied by data-packed tables. For example, the entry **Nirenberg, Marshall Warren**, includes a cross-reference to the **Nobel Prizewinners** table in the Fact-Index, and a citation in **Nixon, Richard M.**, directs the reader to the Fact-Index table of Nixon's Cabinet and Supreme Court appointments. **Nitrogen** contains a table, **Properties of Nitrogen**.

Once you understand how the index works, you will find the entries in the index easy to use. This entry from *Compton's* Fact-Index shows the listing under the subject "*Challenger* Space Shuttle." There are three articles that mention the *Challenger*—one under the heading NASA, one under space travel, and one mention of a reference to the *Challenger* in an article about the United States. The space travel article includes a table. ▶

> **"Challenger"**, space shuttle
> NASA **16**:22
> space travel, *picture* **22**:455, *table* **22**:479
> United States **24**:185

A look at the portion of the NASA ▼
article in Vol. 16 that talks about
the *Challenger* explosion shows that
the reference is quite brief.

> Since it was founded, NASA has had many striking successes and at least two unfortunate tragedies. In 1961 Alan Shepard was the first American sent into space. The following year John Glenn became the first American to orbit the Earth. The most stunning achievement was putting two men on the moon in July 1969. The agency's first major accident was the death by fire in 1967 of astronauts Virgil Grissom, Ed White, and Roger Chaffee. **The second disaster was the explosion of the *Challenger* space shuttle on Jan. 28, 1986. Less than two minutes after lift-off all seven astronauts aboard were killed, including Christa McAuliffe, the first teacher-astronaut.**

Different encyclopedias will have different types and amounts of information. Search in several sets to make sure you have the most complete account of the event. You will also want to check the shelves for any specialized encyclopedias, such as *An Encyclopedia of World History* or *Encyclopedia of World Facts.*

While some libraries still rely heavily on bound encyclopedias, more and more schools are using electronic encyclopedias on CD-ROM. They are interesting to use because they not only allow you to see the text, but have sound and video clips. They also allow for a variety of search strategies: you may do a word search, an idea search, or a topic search. Some allow you to create custom made charts and graphs using statistics found in the program.

Use the power of the computer to help you search. You can:

enter a search word or phrase, (Browse);

begin with the broad category and follow a path that narrows to a focused topic, (Hierarchical);

connect ideas with "and," "or," and "not," (Boolean).

If there is a printer available, you can print out the information you need. You may also be able to copy or download part of the article for use in your report. Remember to cite the source of this information when you use it.

CAUTION Don't be tempted to let a program do your work for you. Remember, the word is research—which means "to search again." If you rely on one source, even a very good one, you are simply copying what someone has already done. Not only is that poor research, it's illegal!

So before you start the download or make a trip to the photo-copier— a word about intellectual property. Intellectual property is something that is a product of the human mind *(intellect)* that has a commercial value, in other words something that someone has created to sell to you and to other people. Since this kind of property is different from a bike or a car, for example, we have created special rules to define and protect it. These are the trademark, patent and copyright laws.

The type of intellectual property law that applies to the encyclopedia article you just found or to the great paper on your topic that you have downloaded from the Web is **copyright law.** This law protects all types of original creative work: music; art, from paintings to photographs to maps; computer software; and *writing*.

So what's protected? Well, the ideas in that article or paper you have can't be copyrighted, *but* the literal form the expressive work takes is. For example, the idea of writing about the *Challenger* disaster cannot be copyrighted. Many people have written about it. But, the actual words and sentences used by an individual in writing a story or book or article or Web page definitely are protected.

How does this happen? To protect something that is printed and sold, like a book, most authors "register" the item with the Library of Congress Copyright Office by sending a copy, together with an application form and fee. However, you don't have to register an item to have copyright protection; any piece of writing is automatically copyrighted the minute it is put to paper. *That includes your work!* No one can use your work without your permission. You can even add the phrase "Copyright ©" followed by the year you wrote the report and your name to notify others that your work is protected. The copyright symbol "©" is internationally recognized, and copyright is protected throughout the world under reciprocal treaties. For most works copyright protection lasts for the lifetime of the author plus fifty years. *Plagiarism,* using someone else's words in your work as if they were your own, can have very serious consequences, including a black mark on your academic record.

Use all the best tools at your fingertips, but use them wisely. In the next chapter we'll take a look at some other electronic resources.

Using Electronic Resources

In this chapter we'll take a closer look two electronic resources that have already been mentioned: CD-ROM and the Internet. These are both good information sources to use when researching events.

CD-ROM New CD-ROMs are being produced all the time; many quite specialized. For example, there is a CD entitled *Seven Days in August* which tells the story of the erection of the Berlin Wall in 1961 to stop a flood of defections from Germany to the West.

Time Almanac 1990s Of special interest to students researching events may be the CD-ROM program *Time Almanac 1990s*. It contains the full text of *Time* magazine. An expanded version is ***Time Almanac Reference Edition*** which contains selected *Time* articles and related historical video clips from the turn of the century through the 1980s.

USA Today: The '90s (Vol.1 &2) This tool contains the newspaper's full-text articles. Again, this CD is limited to events of the 1990s. Also, because *USA Today* specializes in short articles, you won't find the depth of information that you can find in other sources.

For new CDs you will want to check a guide such as *CD-ROM Superguide* by Mike Langberg (Ballantine, 1995), or *CD-ROMs in Print* (Gale, annual). You might even find one whole CD devoted to your chosen topic!

INTERNET Another important electronic resource is the Internet. Earlier, in chapter 5, I described the Internet as a superhighway for information; there you'll find hundreds of thousands of sites on every topic you can imagine. If you can find one site of interest to you, there is a good chance that it will have links to others on the same topic. Unfortunately, these won't always have the information you want—and it may not be as direct as some of the other searches we've already discussed. But chances are you'll learn something you didn't know before and have a good time doing it.

> **To get started:** To use the Web, you need access through browser software, most likely either Netscape or Microsoft Internet Explorer. Ask your school media specialist about Internet access and any policies regarding student use.

Using the Web

The first page of a Web site is the home page. This, along with the other pages, make up a Web site. To search the Web for a specific site, you need the site's address, which is called the "Uniform Resource Locator" (URL). Enter the URL into the Internet browser and the software will take you there. Some libraries have "bookmarked" popular sites to permit faster access. The bookmark is a feature on many browsers that allows the URL of the sites you visit to be saved, so that you don't have to type to same URL over and over again.

Alleyside Press Home Page

← → ⊗ ⌂

URL: http://www.alleyside.com/

■ ■ ■ ■

URL Location

Search Engines

Of course, much of the time you won't have a URL already in mind. Then your search begins with a **search engine.** These are very powerful computers that will search for Web sites by subject, names, or terms. There are many search engines, but the following are among the most popular:

Yahooligans   www.yahooligans.com/   *A search engine designed for kids*

Alta Vista   www.altavista.digital.com/

Infoseek   www.infoseek.com/

Webcrawler   www.webcrawler.com/

Each search engine you use will find a different set of sites

Unlike the catalog in your library, which provides a list of the items in the library using just one system, the Internet has lots of different systems for organization, and there is no one listing that even tries to include everything. Plus, thousands of things are added and deleted every day.

To get started, try a search with the engines listed here, adding others that you may have heard about. Each search engine will produce a slightly different list of Web sites using the same search terms. In time you'll learn which engines you are most comfortable with and will use them most of the time. Until then, it is important to look at the rules for entering search terms in each one you try. There are important differences that you need to know in order to get the most out of your searches.

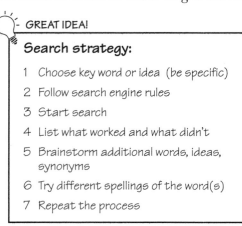

GREAT IDEA!

Search strategy:

1 Choose key word or idea (be specific)

2 Follow search engine rules

3 Start search

4 List what worked and what didn't

5 Brainstorm additional words, ideas, synonyms

6 Try different spellings of the word(s)

7 Repeat the process

Plan on extra time spent following links that aren't on your topic, but that you just can't resist checking out.

Anyone can publish items on the Internet—and many people do for a variety of reasons. Some publish to sell products. Others, who may or may not be authorities on special subjects, want to share information or make statements about causes they care about. Still others write simply to be funny or outrageous—or even to get a job! Since that is the case, not every source that turns up in your search will be reliable. You will have to make judgements about the sources you find. These lists will help you evaluate sites.

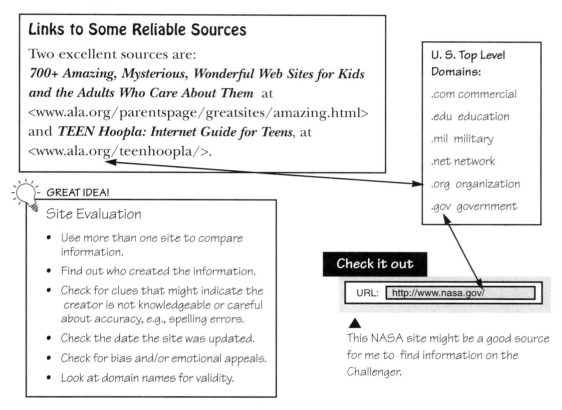

Links to Some Reliable Sources

Two excellent sources are:

700+ Amazing, Mysterious, Wonderful Web Sites for Kids and the Adults Who Care About Them at
<www.ala.org/parentspage/greatsites/amazing.html>
and *TEEN Hoopla: Internet Guide for Teens*, at
<www.ala.org/teenhoopla/>.

U. S. Top Level Domains:

.com commercial

.edu education

.mil military

.net network

.org organization

.gov government

GREAT IDEA!

Site Evaluation

- Use more than one site to compare information.
- Find out who created the information.
- Check for clues that might indicate the creator is not knowledgeable or careful about accuracy, e.g., spelling errors.
- Check the date the site was updated.
- Check for bias and/or emotional appeals.
- Look at domain names for validity.

Check it out

URL: http://www.nasa.gov/

This NASA site might be a good source for me to find information on the Challenger.

Here today, gone tomorrow.

When you find a great page, it's a good idea to make sure you have all the information you need on your first visit. Unlike a library or media center where books remain on the shelves unless they are being used, the "books" can disappear from the Web with the stroke of a Webmaster's delete key. That means the item may no longer be there if you need to go back and take a second look. For that reason, in addition to taking good notes, you should save any documents that you use to a disk or print them out for future reference.

The Internet is a good way to uncover unusual sources. It is also a good—and fun—way to share your ideas with others who have an interest in your topic.

There are also rules for safety and good manners to follow. If anything comes up on the Internet that you are unsure about, or that makes you uneasy, report it to an adult. These issues become more important if you have access to email and extend your research to direct communication with sources you find on the Web.

Using Historical Chronologies

A chronology is a listing of events in the order of their occurrence. You'll find them especially useful for researching your event, and, since you know the date of your event, you'll have no trouble finding the listing in a chronology.

There are many different chronologies, so I've chosen just a few of the most popular to describe here:

Chronology of the Modern World 1763 to the Present Time by Neville Williams (Simon & Schuster, 1995) is a comprehensive dictionary of significant dates in history. It is especially interesting in that it shows the events in their immediate historical perspective. It includes cross references that may help direct you to still other sources.

Easy to use with side tabs for years, *Our Times The Illustrated History of the 20th Century* edited by Lorraine Glennon (Turner Publishing Inc., 1995) is broken into topic headings which include films, art, diplomacy, business, etc. It also has color plates.

Great Events from History edited by Frank Magill (Salem Press) is an excellent multi-volume resource. Each entry is listed with a headline capsule of the event, followed by the date, locale, category, and clear summary of the event. Additional readings are listed as well.

The Day by Day Series (Facts-On-File, Inc.) is a popular chronology that provides a quick reference to specific events. Each decade is covered separately as in *Day by Day: The Forties, Day by Day: the Fifties* and so on. A two-page yearly summary of events is given for each year and then both a monthly and daily chronology of events is listed. The events are listed in ten different subject areas which include World War II, U.S. Politics and Social Issues, Economy and Environment, Science and Technology, Culture, Leisure and Lifestyle.

The Twentieth Century: An Almanac (World Almanac Publications) is divided into eight sections each focusing on key events. It contains 253 illustrations and maps.

Current Affairs Atlas (Facts on File), covers more than 50 topics. This reference guide is a little different from the others in that it looks at currents, or trends, in history that shape the world and provide today's headlines.

A huge chronology, *The People's Chronology. A Year-by-Year Record of Human Events from Prehistory to the Present* edited by James Trager (Henry Holt, 1996), includes 30,000 entries. Even more comprehensive is the 1,292 page *Chronicle of the World*, edited by Jerome Burne (Prentice-Hall). With colored plates and maps, it covers the time from 3.5 million years B.C. to 1945.

There are many, many others. Because they cover so wide a span of time and include many events, the articles probably will not be in depth. But they are good sources for checking dates and basic facts.

Next we will look at a variety of other sources you will want to explore as you do your research.

Using Other Sources

There are still a few other resources you should investigate before you consider your library research finished.

Almanacs are collections of facts and statistics. They are usually published annually. Use them to confirm statistics that you have uncovered in other sources.

Atlases are books of maps, geographic and political information. Make sure you use them to locate where your event occurred. Knowing the global setting of the event will deepen your understanding of it.

Audiobooks, films, video, and laser disks may provide you with a perspective you would not find anywhere else—and can make your report unique.

Just as you must be careful when selecting materials found on the Internet, you must also view these audio-visual resources with a critical eye. The producers may "stretch" the facts a little to make the audio-visual more entertaining. Check the credits at the beginning or end of the audio-visual to see if the content is based on solid sources of information. Consider also the purpose and intent of the producers. Who is the intended audience? For example, a National Geographic production on the *Challenger* explosion would have a different purpose than a Hollywood production of the same event. Which do you think would be the more reliable source of factual information?

Go there. Visit points of interest, uncover nuggets of information in out-of-the way places, and interview eyewitnesses to make your project an exciting one that will be interesting to read.

Narrative vs Documentary Histories

It's important for the student of history—and that's what you are when you research historical events —to understand the difference between narrative history and documentary history.

Narrative history is a description of past events based on accounts written by one, or at the most, a few people. These secondary sources are the kinds of accounts you would find in history textbooks, encyclopedias, chronicles, and so on.

Documentary history, on the other hand, is written by people who lived through the event. They are writing about what was happening at the moment. What better source can there be than a report from someone who was actually there and experienced the event first-hand?

> An excellent source of documentary history is a massive work entitled ***The Annals of America** (Encyclopedia Britannica)*. This nineteen volume work contains 2289 selections including speeches, editorials, diaries, fiction, poems, and transcriptions of dialogues and conversations that occurred during the time events were taking place. It is unlikely that you will find this work in your school library. It is well worth your while to try to locate it at a public or university library.

GREAT IDEA!

Earlier we mentioned using indexes to locate primary sources such as newspaper and magazine articles, but sometimes a nugget will turn up in unexpected places. In an article in a local newspaper entitled "Spaced Out" I found this gem. The author of the article asked a number of people the question, "When did you first become interested in the space program?" She reported:

> "The day I really got into it was the day the *Challenger* blew up (Jan. 28, 1986). I was in high school watching it on TV," said Palmer, 28. When the artist's assistant describes having several times, from her Bradenton home, witnessed a shuttle slash across the sky, from Florida's east coast to the west, the awe is faint, yet apparent. "You could see the orange flame, and the trail it left behind." When asked what she thought when she saw the burnished streak, Palmer said, "I just wondered what was going through their minds." (Cubarrubia, Eydie. "Are We Spaced Out?" Bradenton Herald. [August 31, 1997] People Section, page 3, column 3.)

Sometimes things will even turn up in the Letters to the Editor column. Look at this excerpt from a first hand account of the end World War II. Wouldn't this account add a wonderful human interest touch to a research report on the final days of World War II?

> **WWII end: a memorable day**
> EDITOR: Thursday was the 52nd anniversary of the end of World War II, and it brought back memories of one of the most exciting nights of my life. I was 20 in my hometown of Racine, Wis. There had been several false alarms about the war ending, which really drove us crazy. People were hugging their radios for three days, but finally it was here—it was now, it was happening—the day millions had prayed for and dreamed about for almost four long years! ... Everybody in town was there. Confetti and toilet paper were flying all over. Cars had stopped trying to get through Main Street and just parked and honked their horns. Snake dances were winding in and out of the stores. Boys were throwing girls into the pool on the Square. Factory whistles were blowing. The celebrating went on all night, or so we heard later.
> (Clark, June. "Letter to the Editor." Bradenton Herald. [August 17, 1997] Editorial page 4.)

Journals and diaries are other good primary sources. Look for them in the history room at the public library or archive. A visit to the archives can be very exciting; like taking a walk back through time with historical figures.

Interviews are special, too. Talking with someone who actually experienced the event you are researching will add life to the event for you, and to your report. Be sure to prepare a list of questions beforehand. This will make you appear professional and prepared, plus you'll have the written questions, just in case you get nervous during the interview. Tape recording the interview makes note-taking unnecessary.

Museums, historical societies, and park services are excellent sources of information. Not long ago, I was researching an event for a historical novel. While visiting the historical society in the town where the event took place, I spent hours and hours leafing through the paper files. To my delight, I discovered a letter written by one of the key figures describing in great detail the event that took place nearly 100 years ago. I felt like a miner who had struck gold!

Searching these out-of-the-way sources will take lots of time and patience, but they will uncover wonderful tidbits of information. And these bits of information will set your paper apart and make it stand out as a quality piece of research. It's also what makes your research journey a memorable one!

Taking Notes

Taking good notes and using the information well is the key to writing an effective research paper. **There are three ways to take notes: taking down direct quotes, paraphrasing, and summarizing.**

Direct Quotes

If you come across an **especially well-written powerful statement** like the one here, you would do well to quote it directly. Since this is a short quote, quotation marks are used:

> "The relatives are now left to cope with the sight that has linked strangers in grief: seven people at the pinnacle of their lives, riding a symbol of national achievement in a disintegrating fireball." (Jay Hamburg, Orlando Sentinel, Feb. 9, 1986. Page A-16)

You also want to use a direct quote for **material that is complex.** Paraphrasing would be difficult or might make the meaning less clear, as in this description of McAuliffe's assignment taken from the *U.S. Presidential Commission on the Space Shuttle Challenger Accident Report to the President.* Since the quote is longer than four lines, it is indented and typed single-spaced.

> McAuliffe's assignment was to demonstrate and explain the effects of microgravity (free fall in orbit) in the context of Newtonian physics and the scientific, commercial, and industrial applications of space flight. She would address an audience of school children via television from the spaceship.

Paraphrasing and Summarizing

Lengthy articles are best paraphrased or summarized. In paraphrasing, the information is put in your own words using one or several lines of information. In summarizing, you condense the main points in the article, again using your own words. Let's see how this works by both paraphrasing and summarizing the following information from *Challenger, The Final Voyage:*

 GREAT IDEA!
Written material may be photocopied and highlighted for later use.

> The abort system was contingent on main engine failure. There was no abort system planned against failure of one or both solid rocket boosters during the first two minutes of the ascent. Nor was there any means of escape for the crew. Unlike Mercury, Gemini, and Apollo spacecraft, the orbiter was not equipped with a launch escape system during the solid rocket booster phase, the first stage of the ascent. Such a system had been considered during the development of the shuttle, but had been dropped, except for the temporary installation of aircraft-style ejection seats in Columbia, because failure of the solid rocket boosters after launch was considered highly improbable. (Lewis, Richard S. *Challenger, The Final Voyage*. New York: Columbia University Press, 1988. p.3.)

A paraphrase of the information might look like this: Neither an abort system nor a means of escape for the crew was planned. Because an abort system is based on main engine failure and it was considered highly unlikely that the solid rocket boosters would fail after launch, the orbiter did not have a launch escape system during the first stage of the ascent.

A summarization would look like this: Abort systems are based on the potential of main engine failure. Since it was considered unlikely that that one or both solid rocket boosters would fail, there was no plan in place against the failure of the boosters during the first two minutes of the flight. Although Mercury, Gemini, and Apollo space craft were equipped with a launch escape system, there was no means of escape for the crew of the Challenger during the solid rocket booster phase. A considered plan was rejected because it was not thought probable that such a failure of the rocket boosters would occur.

When you are planning to paraphrase or summarize information in your report, it is best
to do your note-taking in key phrase or word notes that will make it easier for you to put
the notes in your own words when you are writing
the report. For example, a note card of this
information might look something like this: ▶

> Abort system for main engine failure. None for failure of
> rocket boosters during first two minutes.
>
> No way for crew to escape. Mercury, Gemini, and Apollo had
> launch escape system during sold rocket booster stage; not
> Challenger. Considered but dropped. Thought failure of solid
> rocket booters highly unlikely.
>
> Lewis, <u>The Final Voyage</u>

Giving Credit to Your Sources.
No matter whether you use a direct
quote, paraphrase, or summarize, you must give credit to your sources by citing
the references that you use. You may show your sources of information in one
of three ways: footnotes, endnotes, or parenthetical documentation. Your
teacher will tell you which way you are to use in your report.

Footnotes.
Footnotes are exactly what the word suggests—notes found at the
foot of the page. Footnotes are numbered in the order the documented material appears on the pages of the report. For example, the direct quote mentioned earlier would be documented like this in the report: ▼

```
"The relatives are now left to cope with the sight that has
linked strangers in grief: seven people at the pinnacle of
their lives, riding a symbol of national achievement in a
disintegrating fireball."¹

1. Hamburg, Jay. Orlando Sentinel, Feb. 9, 1986, p. A-16.)
                                                        -2
```

> The small number at the end of the
> quote lets the reader know that the
> information came from another source
> and points him to the footnote to
> learn the source of the information.

If later in the report you used information from the same source again, you don't have to
retype the entire footnote. You simply use the author's last name, the Latin word op. cit.,
which means "in the work cited," and the page number for the new information. Like this: ▼

```
5. Hamburg, op. cit., p. 6.
```

Sometimes you use information from the
same source two times in a row. In that
case, it's even easier. You use the Latin
word ibid., meaning "in the same place," and
give the page number this way: ▶

```
6. Ibid., p.8.
```

If you use footnotes to document your sources, you will make a bibliography to
place at the end of your report. The bibliography lists in alphabetical order all
the sources you used in preparing your paper, including the ones that you read
for background information, but didn't actually use in your report.

Parenthetical Documentation. Parenthetical documentation is another way of citing the sources of your information. This is an easier way than using footnotes because you simply put your source in parenthesis right after the information you are using. For example: ▼

```
". . .riding a symbol of national achievement in a disintegrating
fireball" (Hamburg, Jay. Orlando Sentinel, Feb. 9, 1986).
```

When you use parenthetical documentation, you will prepare a References or Works Cited page, listing in alphabetical order only the sources you actually cited in your paper. This, like a bibliography, will be placed at the end of your report.

End Notes. A third way to document your sources is with the use of endnotes. Here you use numbers in the text just as you would for footnotes, but instead of putting the documentation at the bottom of the pages, you list the notations at the end of your paper. You write the endnotes just like you would for footnotes and again you write a bibliography.

No matter which form of documentation you use, you must give the page numbers for each source cited. Be sure to put down the page numbers when you are taking your notes. There's nothing worse than having to go back to the library to search through sources looking for missing numbers.

Bibliography

When you are all finished with the writing of your paper, you will prepare the bibliography or reference page. The bibliography is a listing of all the materials you have used for your report. Because this is a collection of a variety of kinds of sources, you will use a different way of recording the bibliographical information for each.

Subject books are listed with **author's name first**, followed by the title of the book, the city of publication, the name of the publisher and the date of publication.

```
Lewis, Richard S. Challenger: The Final Voyage. New York:
Columbia University Press, 1988.
```

Reference book entries begin with the last name of the author of the article if one is given. Often the author's name is not given. If it isn't, you list the **title of the article first**, then the name of the reference book, city, publisher, date of publication, and page number. The *Compton Encyclopedia* article would be listed like this.

```
"National Aeronautics and Space Administration (NASA)."
Compton's Encyclopedia. Chicago, IL: Encyclopedia
Britannica, 1991, p.22.
```

Periodical articles are entered by the author's last name first when the author is identified:

> Casey, Kathryn. "Remembering the Challenger." <u>Ladies Home Journal</u>. Vol.113, Jan.,1996.

If **no author's name** is given, use the title of the article first, then the rest of the bibliographical information:

> "Space Shuttle Challenger." Time Magazine. February 10, 1986.

If your source is a **CD-ROM,** you would use the following format :

> Space Travel. CD-ROM. Burbank: Warner New Media. 1996.

Information found on the **Internet** and the World Wide Web (WWW) also needs to be cited. The following are examples of citations for electronic sources:

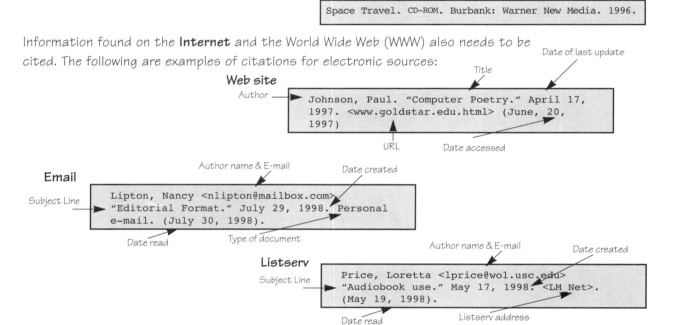

Web site

Author → Johnson, Paul. "Computer Poetry." April 17, 1997. <www.goldstar.edu.html> (June, 20, 1997)

Title — Date of last update — URL — Date accessed

Email

Subject Line → Lipton, Nancy <nlipton@mailbox.com> "Editorial Format." July 29, 1998. Personal e-mail. (July 30, 1998).

Author name & E-mail — Date created — Date read — Type of document

Listserv

Subject Line → Price, Loretta <lprice@wol.usc.edu> "Audiobook use." May 17, 1998. <LM Net>. (May 19, 1998).

Author name & E-mail — Date created — Date read — Listserv address

In preparing your bibliography, it is important to be consistent in the style you use. Your school may provide students with a school-based style manual that shows students exactly how reports should be written and documented and how to write the bibliographical information. Or you may have been given or been asked to purchase one of several commercially prepared style manuals. Most of these, though, have been written for high school and college students and may be difficult for middle school students to use.

The bibliography or reference page is an important part of your research project for several reasons. First, it provides documentation of the sources of your information and provides evidence that you have conducted a thorough investigation. Second, it gives credit to the writers whose work provided the information you used. Finally, the bibliography gives your reader a list of resources if he or she wants to do additional research in the topic area of your report.

This very important part of your paper must be prepared just as carefully as the body of your report.

Putting It All Together

Now that you have gathered your information, you need to decide how to organize it. Your outline will be helpful at this point. Examine each notecard to see where it will fit in the general outline. Label the notes to correspond with the outline, adding new main ideas where necessary.

Graphic organizers are also helpful in sorting out your ideas. Creating a **web** similar to the one discussed in chapter 2 is another way to organize your

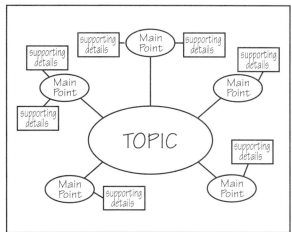

research in preparation to writing your paper. The center of the web contains the research topic. Branching out from the topic are the main points you plan to make and from each main point, supporting details for that idea.

Others prefer to arrange their note cards in the form of a **chart**. This method makes rearranging information easy and gives you a visual of the big picture.

Time lines are especially useful tools for organizing information about events. The note cards can be laid out chronologically along the time line. As you write your paper, you will relate the events in the order they happened. Timelines also allow you to see cause and effect relationships.

With all the research complete, you are ready now to be creative. Remember, the event itself is not of your creation, nor are the facts and the information that you have gathered creative. In fact, they had better not be or you'll be in big trouble with your teacher!

But the way you present the information will be uniquely your own. The reader should be able to hear your voice and catch your enthusiasm for the project. It should make him or her want to learn even more about the event.

You must, of course, be sure that you have met the teacher's requirements for the paper. After that, you are limited only by your own imagination as to how you might present your information in a unique way.

GREAT IDEA!
If your teacher provides a rubric for evaluation, use it _now!_

You might introduce your topic with the use of a newspaper headline, much as I introduced this book in the first chapter. Then you could present the report as a series of **newspaper articles**. You might write the articles as day-by-day accounts of the unfolding of the event, just as if you were an investigative reporter at the time the event occurred.

Perhaps you could use an **interview** format and describe the event through the eyes of a variety of eyewitnesses to the event. Would they all have the same response to the events even though the facts are unchanging?

Memoirs, and diary or journal entries are still other possibilities. As you become engrossed in the event you are researching, I'm sure you will think of others. Try to choose a way to present the material that will make the reader relive the event with you.

Final Report

Your final report should represent your very best work. No matter how creative or unique your presentation, it will not shine through a report that is messy, error filled, or difficult to read. Be sure to use a dictionary or spell-check on your word processing program to check the accuracy of your spelling. Remember that spell-check can check your spelling, but not the accuracy of your word choice. Then proofread carefully for grammar and usage. It's a good idea to have someone else proofread your next-to-the-last draft. Finding errors in your own work is much more difficult than spotting errors in someone else's.

If at all possible, your report should be typed or printed using a word processing program, such as Microsoft Word or WordPerfect. Otherwise, the report should be written in your best handwriting. Present it attractively in a binder with a title page, your full name, the date that you finished the work and perhaps your school's name.

Evaluation

Now is the time to look back over your research journey and ask yourself some questions. Was your problem solving process and information gathering successful? Were you able to find what you needed? Did the information meet the needs of your original project?

Question yourself about the final product. Does it meet the requirements of the assignment? Did you use a variety of resources and document them properly? Is your presentation creative, attractive and free of errors?

Finally, ask yourself in which parts of the process you were most successful and what, if anything, you would do differently the next time.

When you have retraced your journey and answered these questions, you should be able to prop your feet up and say, "Great trip!"